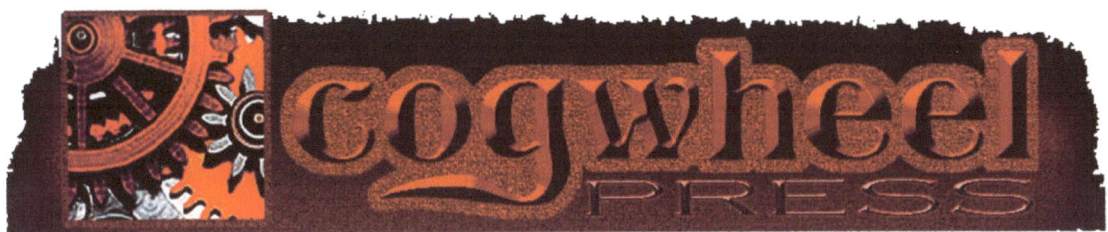

www.CogwheelPress.net

ISBN-13: 978-1511560382

ISBN-10: 151156038X

A Faerie's Guide to Life

Book 1

Enjoy colorful art by Ivy Patrick
and quirky poetry by Desiree Finkbeiner,
combined to create *A Faerie's Guide to Life;*
A unique collection of 12 mini rhyming fantasy
stories for faerie lovers of all ages.
Do you believe in magic?

Contents

Aimer (LOVE)

To love completely is to care so sweetly
for the one who keeps your heart discretely.
To love so truly is to never speak rudely
to the one who values you far above rubies.
To love most fairly is to deal with one squarely
and never another one to compare thee.
For when love is true, there is only you
and never a need to change or subdue.

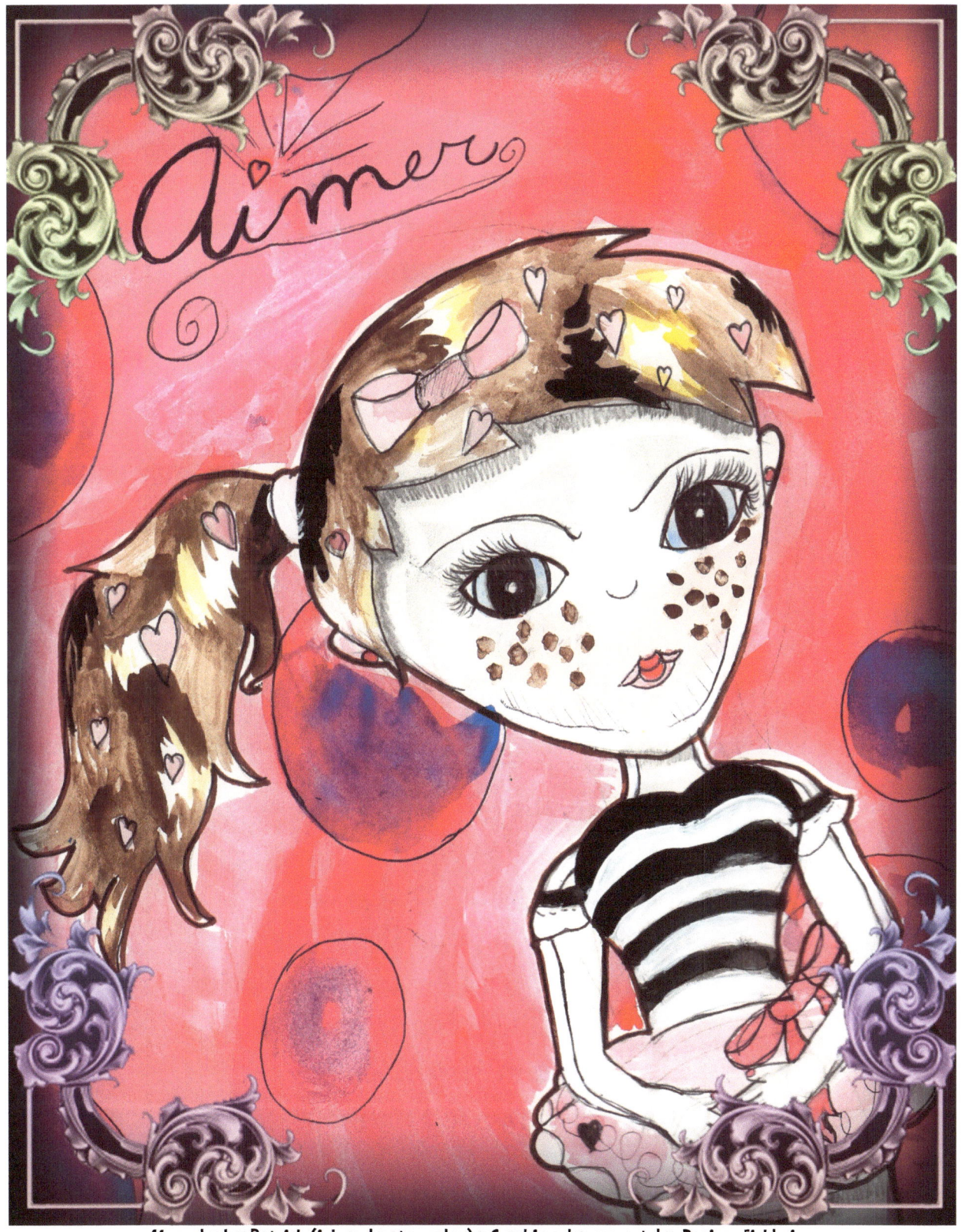

Aimer by Ivy Patrick (ink and water color) = Graphic enhancement by Desiree Finkbeiner

The Archer

I aim to please
and not by degrees
but with exactness
I shoot the breeze...
We're not talking small talk,
`cause I walk the strait walk,
And I make my point with
precise expertise.
Should I miss the bulls eye
when my arrows fly
I'll quickly correct it
again and retry.
To sin is to miss it,
but I hope to hit it,
into the middle of things,
I must admit it.
Draw back your conclusions
shoot through your illusions,
open your mind and be free of confusion!
Your heart is the target
and I aim to please,
so let's seize the moment
and shoot at the breeze...

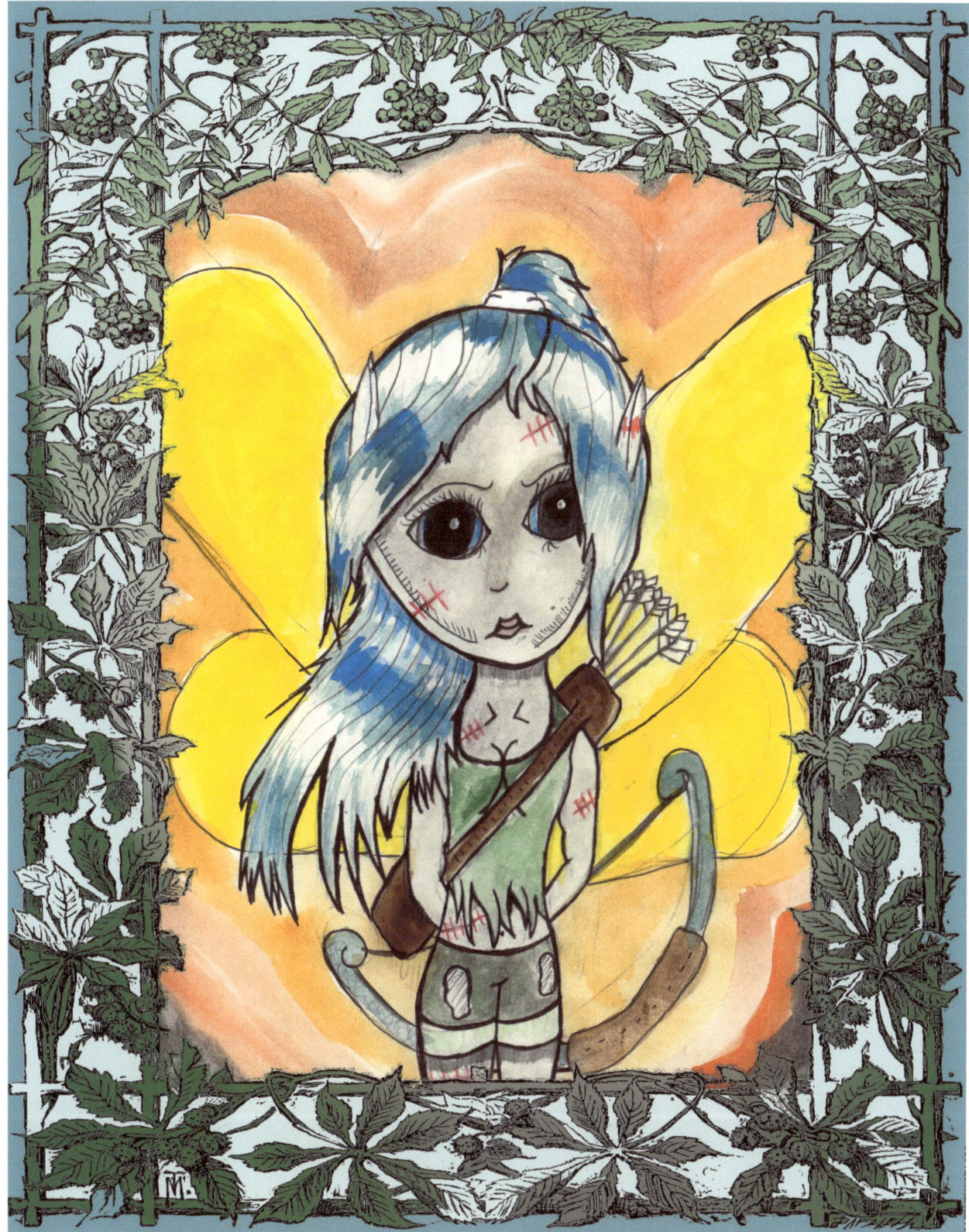

The Archer by Ivy Patrick (ink and water color) = Graphic enhancement by Desiree Finkbeiner

Cupid

Love conquers all,
so I've been told
but how could I know
until I grow old?
For in love is wisdom
but fools will rush in.
The wise are the aged
as ignorance begins.
Give me the experience,
which comes with mistakes
and in my repentance
and foolish heartaches
the wisdom of ages
begins to awake...

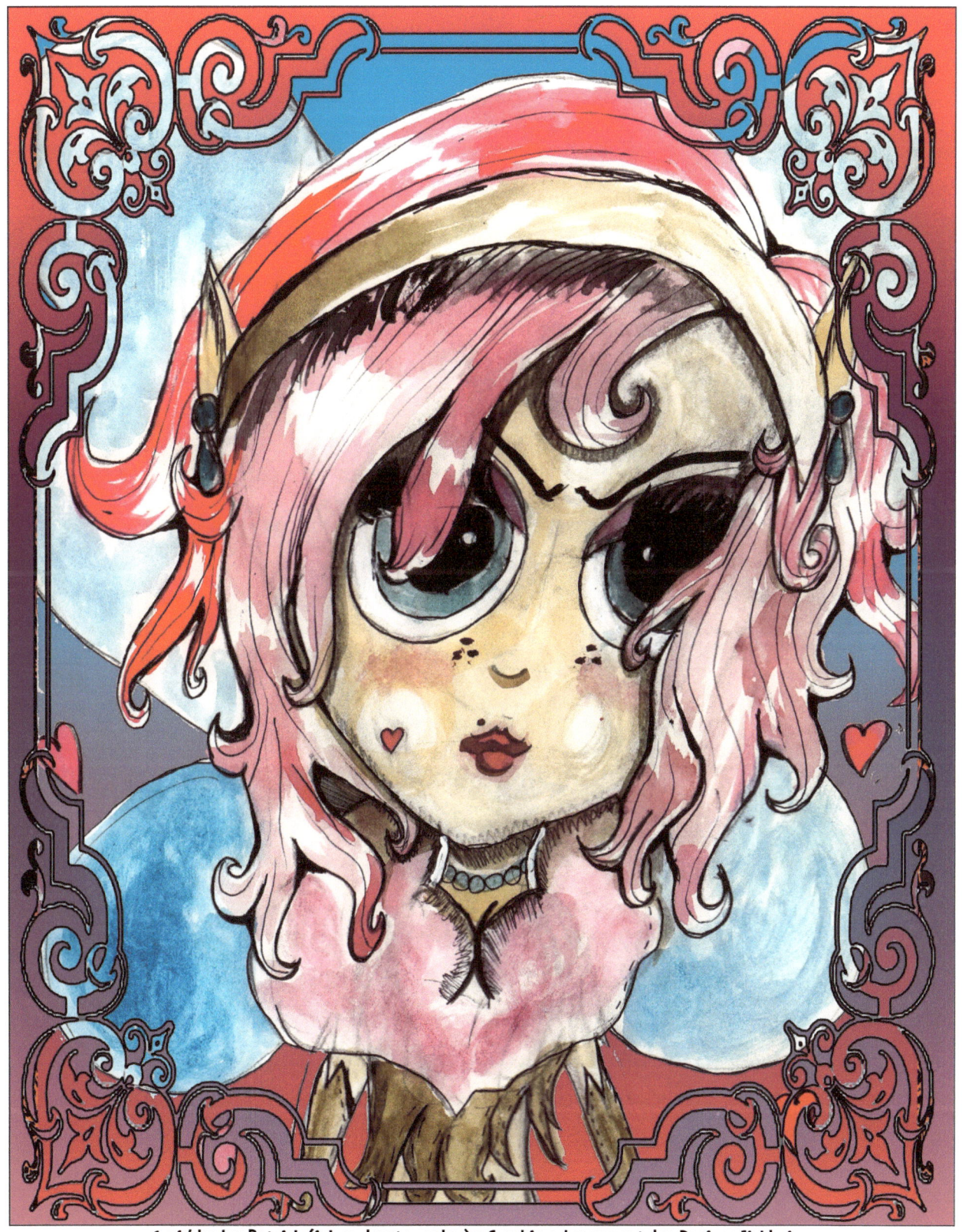

Cupid by Ivy Patrick (ink and water color) = Graphic enhancement by Desiree Finkbeiner

Dragon

Fire breathing thoughts conceiving
pass from doubt into believing
naughty nuisance; never heeding
discipline for all the thieving
hoards of gold and treasure troves
burning up the forest groves
flames of mischief
thief in the night
filling other minds with fright.

Scales of justice to the heart
in the open wound a dart
Dragon, you will not be stealing
any hearts who are believing
sword of justice in my hand
preserver of liberty in the land!

Dragon, you will not be feeling
only humbled hearts are healing
your is callous, cold, and dark
mine is burning with a spark,
for all the fire you spit out
you've an awful lot of doubt.

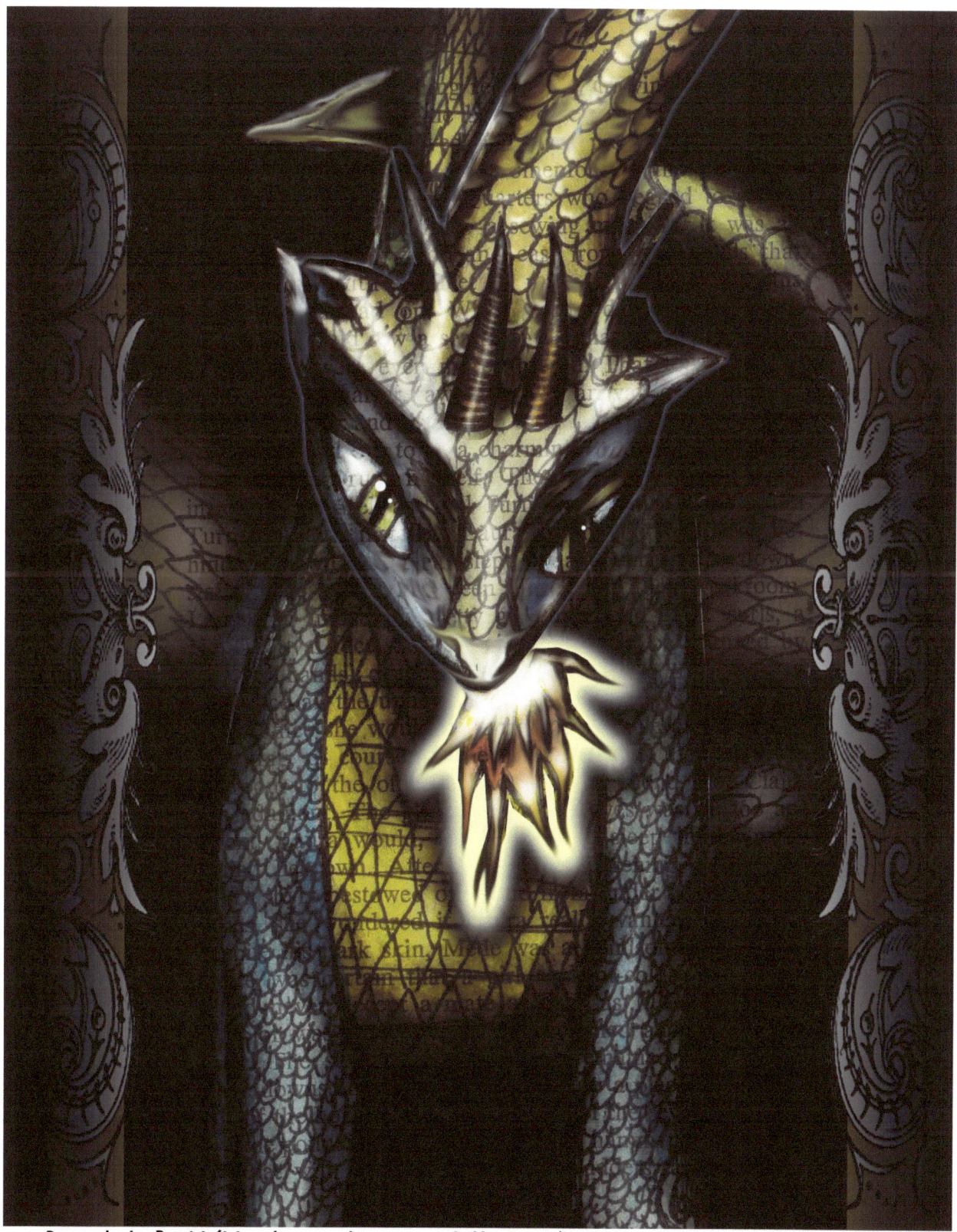

Dragon by Ivy Patrick (ink and water color on a recycled book page) = Graphic enhancement by Desiree Finkbeiner

Fairy God Mother

"I need some advice,
just a thought should suffice
so the lessons in life do not come at great price."
Said the princess of youth,
seeking pearls of deep truth.
And the fairy began, "Avoid substance abuse."
She leaned to her ear,
"And of mischief steer clear,
stay away from the sprites in the forest, my dear.
For they offer a tonic
that a delivers a chronic
case of amnesia and a spell with a sonnet.
They slip in their magic,
and affects can be tragic
for they cause one to change by degrees that are drastic!"
"Oh my" said the princess,
"That does NOT sound delicious!
To become the victim of acts so malicious.
How can I resit
should they persist
in their tempting and luring; how may I desist?"
"Be true to your heart,
and to others impart
of knowledge and good deeds, and of music and art.
And you'll have GOOD friends;
ones that truly defend
your virtue and honor, that will last till the end."

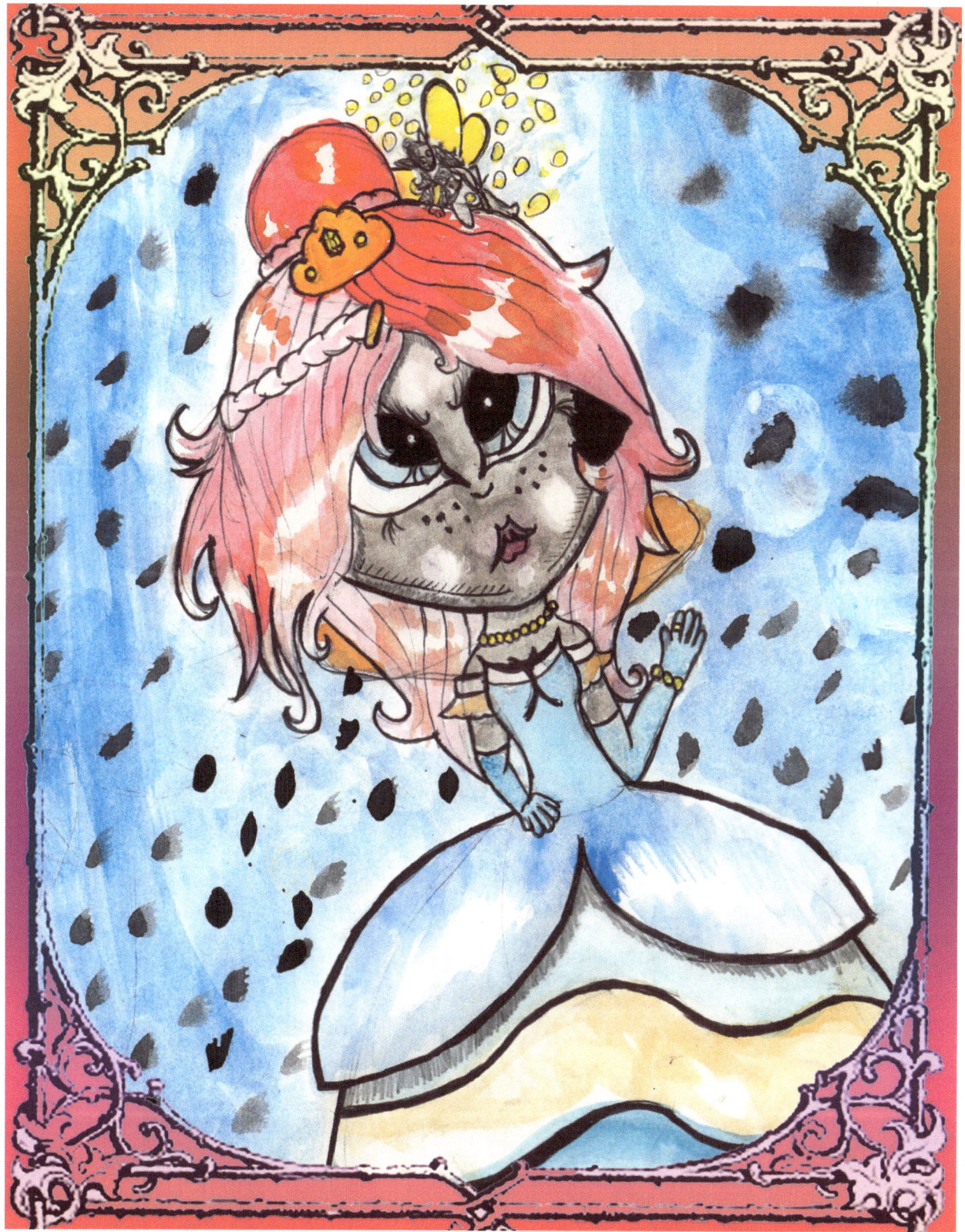

Fairy Godmiother by Ivy Patrick (ink and water color) = Graphic enhancement by Desiree Finkbeiner

Firefly

"Do you grant wishes?" Asked the fly,
to the fairy who flew so high.
"Well that depends," she said with a smile,
"if you can make my time worthwhile.
What have you to offer in exchange,
for me to grant your life some change?"
"I've only my friendship," he offered up,
"for you to fill my empty cup."

"May your wish be granted." And she touched his heart,
"And may we never be apart!
For no gift is nobler than to be a friend
and no better way for my time to spend
than giving the light of my life to another,
who esteems me the same as he would a brother."
The fly felt a change burning deep within,
as he felt their friendship of love begin.

A burning desire to brighten her day,
began to chase his blues away.
For he was illuminated by new light,
and he began to buzz into flight!
He burned brighter as they climbed the sky,
for he had become a firefly!

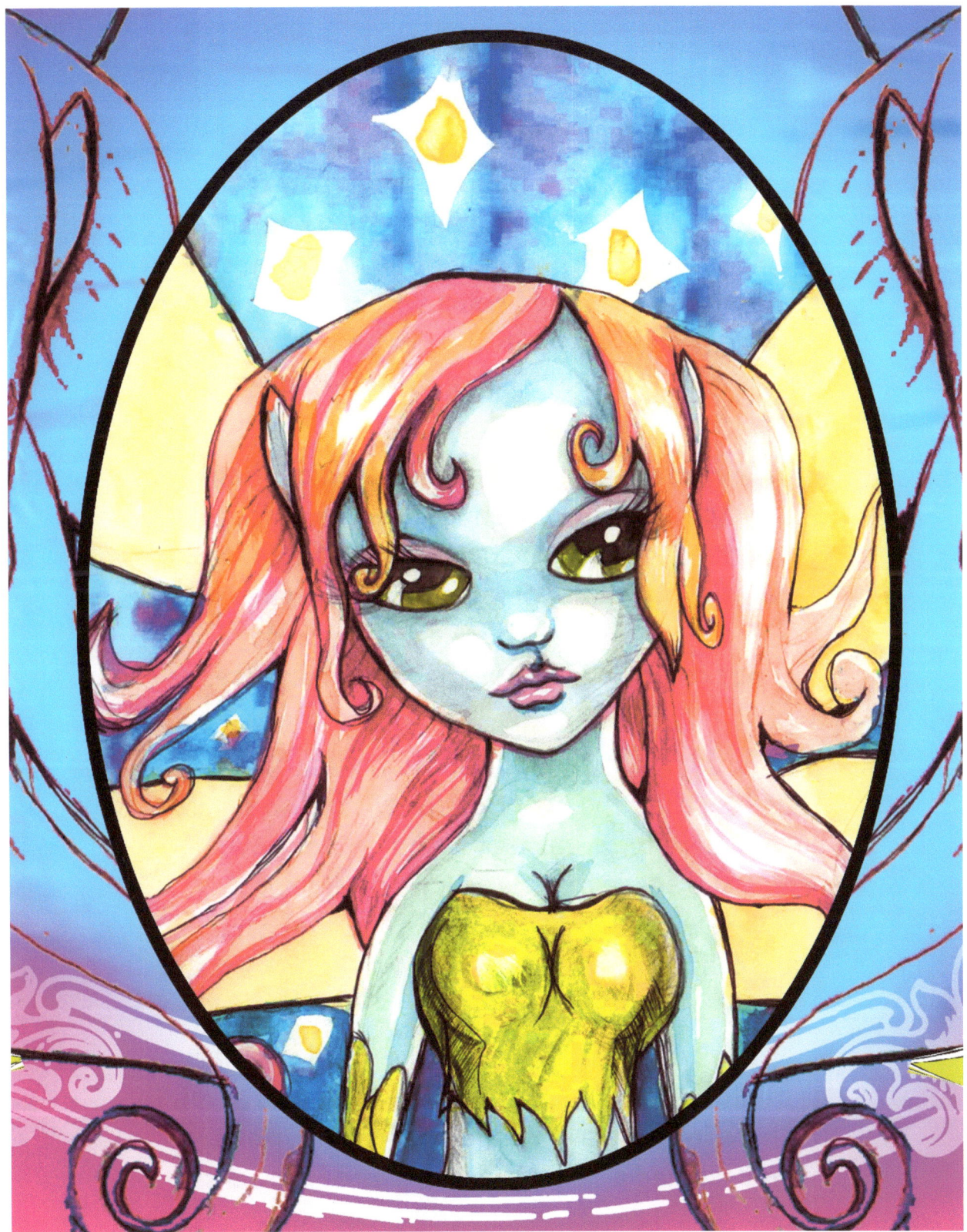

Fire Fairy by Ivy Patrick (ink and water color) = Graphic enhancement by Desiree Finkbeiner

The Gardener

A faerie was born in a cherry plum tree
who had a green thumb and a spirit so free.
And all she touched would blossom, you see,
so the wicked old witch sought to drown her at sea.
She sent out her minions to catch the wee lass,
and they trapped her in a container of glass.

They brought her to that wicked old hag,
who cackled so vile and proceeded to brag,
"I've got the green thumb and I will defeat
all that is wholesome and holy and sweet!"
She opened the jar and reached in to demise,
but could not obliterate to her surprise.

The faerie extended her tiny green thumb,
and touched the heart of the wicked so numb.
Where once was empty, began to grow,
the seeds of love which she did sow.
The wicked old witch fell to the ground,
and ceased to crow with her shrilling sounds...

She crumbled away into the good earth!
Her minions were freed and they giggled with mirth!
There in the grave where she lost her powers,
blossomed a beautiful bouquet of flowers!

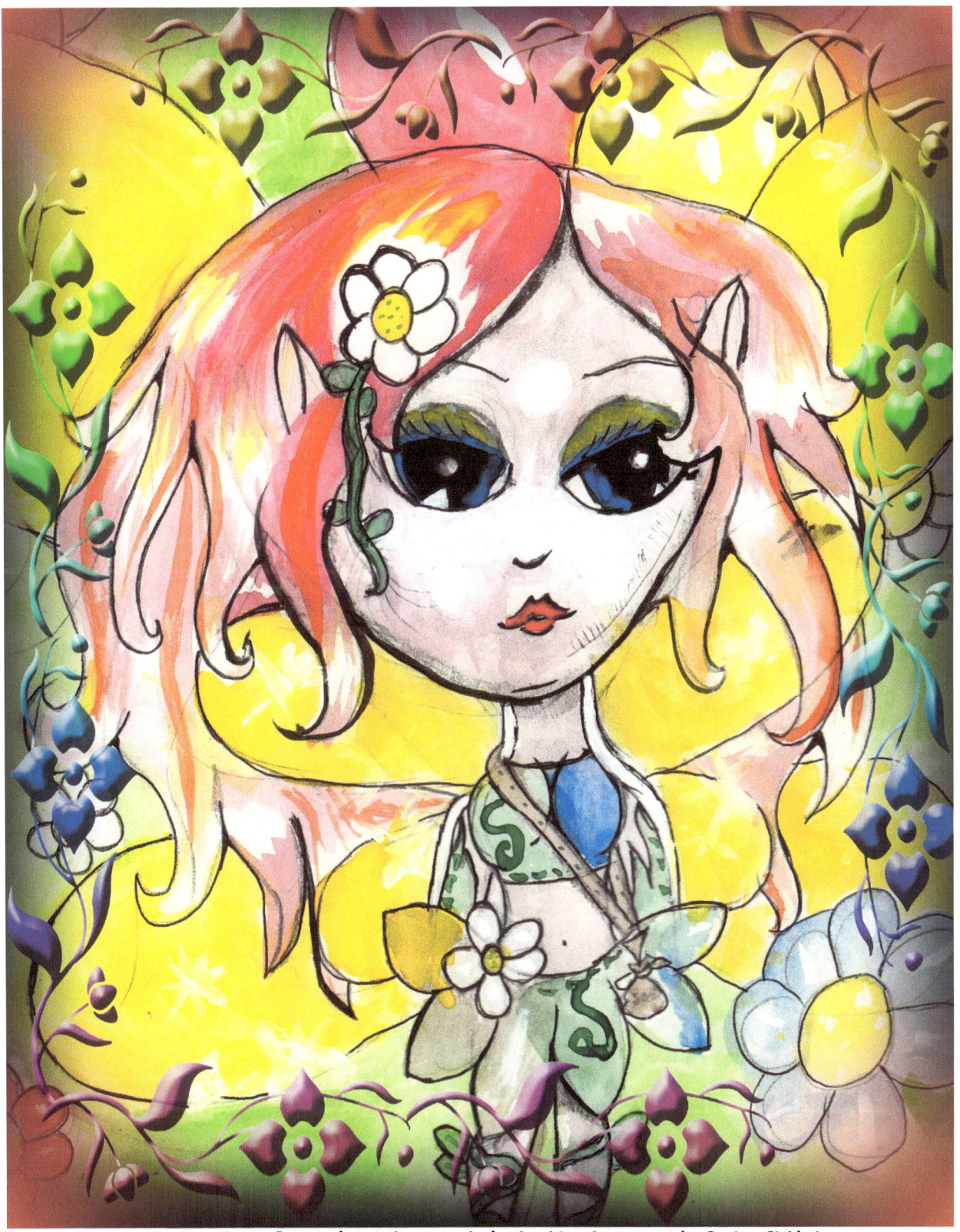

The Gardener by Ivy Patrick (ink and water color) = Graphic enhancement by Desiree Finkbeiner

The General

Generally, I enjoy taking charge
of the vagabond minds who are wandering at large.
For those who cannot decide for themselves,
I gather them up and deliver to elves.

For humans who give in to despicable vice,
do fetch from the elves a considerable price.
Minds of slaves, they have weak wills,
and barter their liberty for cheap thrills.

And I'm the general at their command,
who captures by vice and delivers demands.
Because they are slaves to addictions and wont,
I call them in with a lure; they respond.

But for those who hold true to their principles clear,
I've no power over, for they do adhere
to their own conscious, to will and to choice,
the ones who speak with their own voice.

A word of caution to those who are weak,
who after the pleasures of flesh they do seek,
I will own you, and use you, and sell you at price,
in snares I will catch you by your wicked vice.

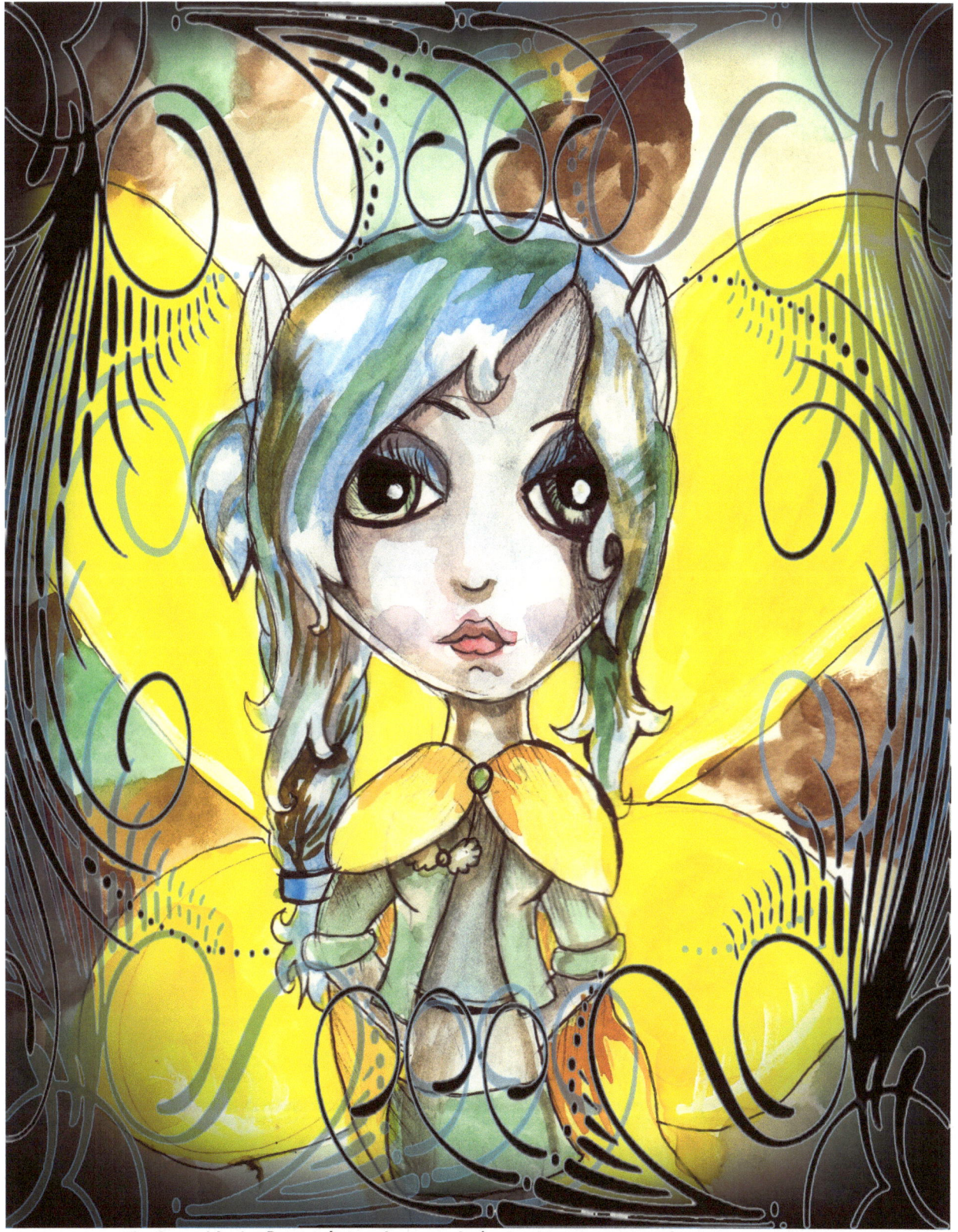

The General by Ivy Patrick (ink and water color) = Graphic enhancement by Desiree Finkbeiner

Golden Mermaid

Cast your nets
and place your bets
we shall see what gambling gets

chances are
not good so far
for gamblers only aid the czar

a one in five
says you will win
alas you pull out empty again

penny for thoughts
on casting lots
for a golden mermaid is highly sought

few that find her
never bind her
allow me to make a gentle reminder:

hearts are never won by chance,
or luck or meager circumstance.
Love is earned and hard to keep
and never comes for free or cheap.

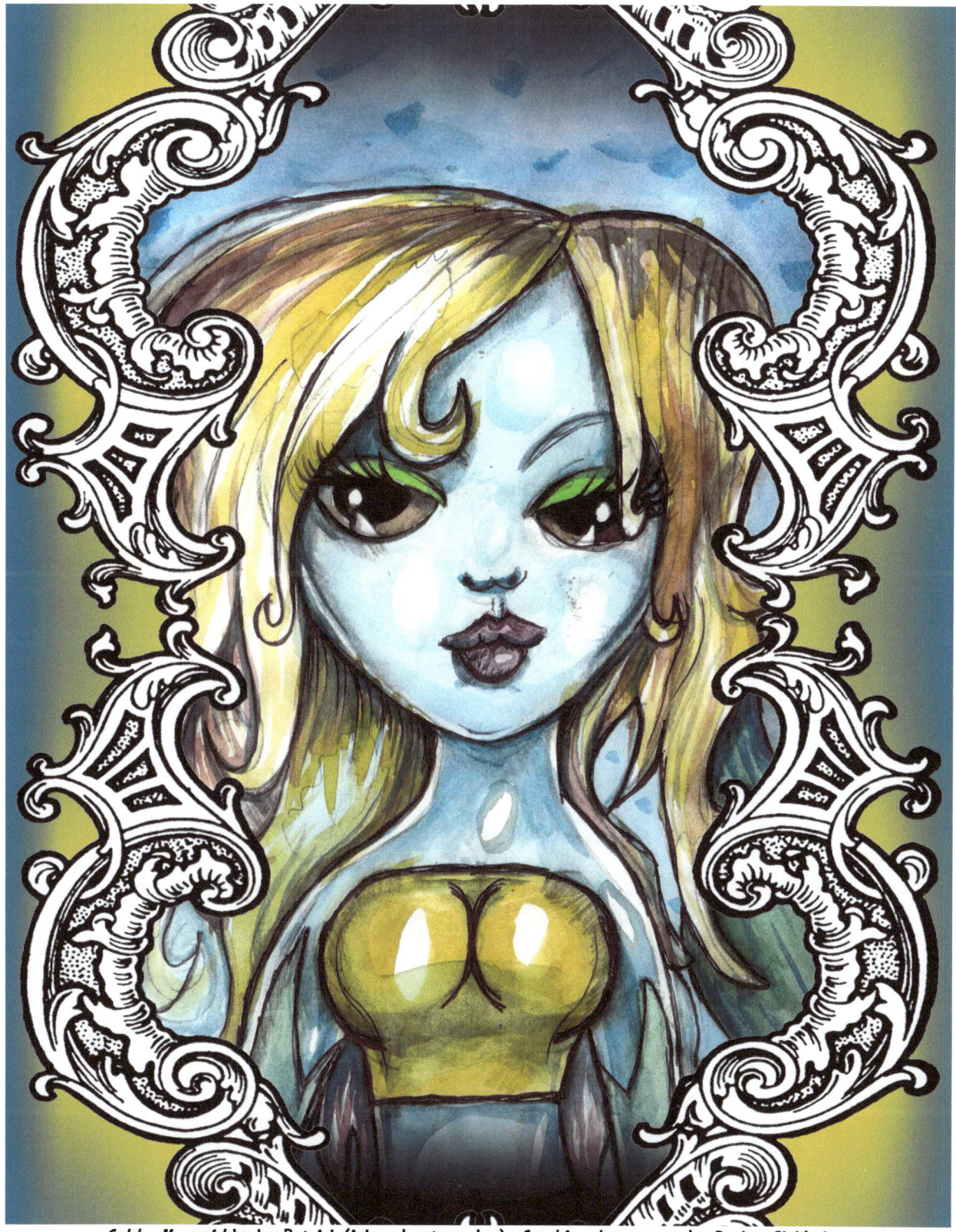

Golden Mermaid by Ivy Patrick (ink and water color) = Graphic enhancement by Desiree Finkbeiner

The Pilot

Fly me into unknown skies!
Navigate without compromise
one direction, towards the goal
never-ceasing self control.

Pilot me to safety's rest,
north and south, from east to west.
Float with me in clouds of white
soaring heavenward in flight!

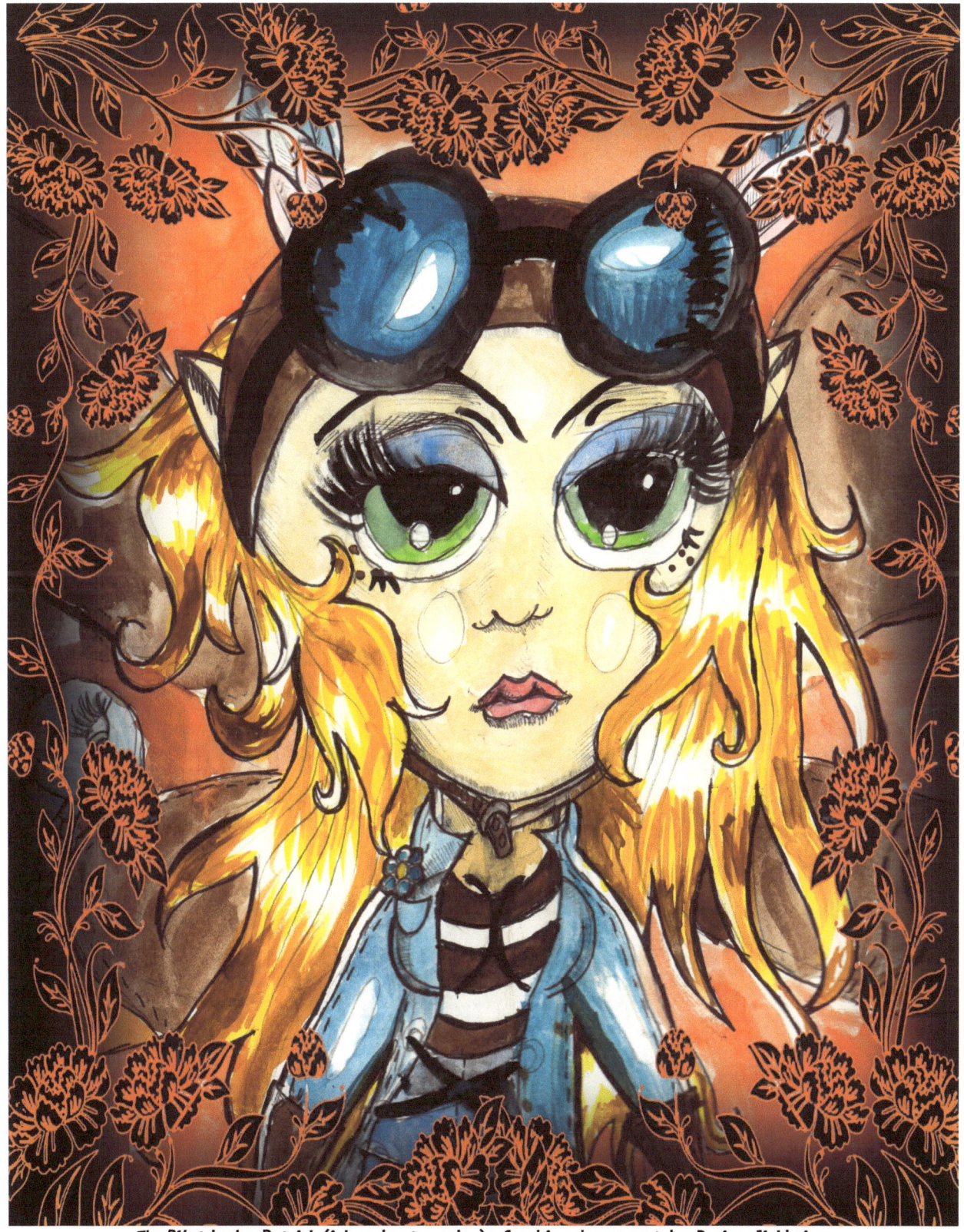

The Pilot by Ivy Patrick (ink and water color) = Graphic enhancement by Desiree Finkbeiner

Punky

Spunky, punky, feeling funky,
fly through the treetops like a monkey.
Snappy, happy, feeling scrappy,
don't talk back or I may slap ye.

Willy nilly, feeling silly,
summer hot and winter chilly,
Tricky, licky sweet and sticky,
ate too much now I feel sicky.

Runny honey in the sunny,
can't buy love with common money.
Blimey! Spiny critter tiny,
stubbed my toe and now I'm whiny.

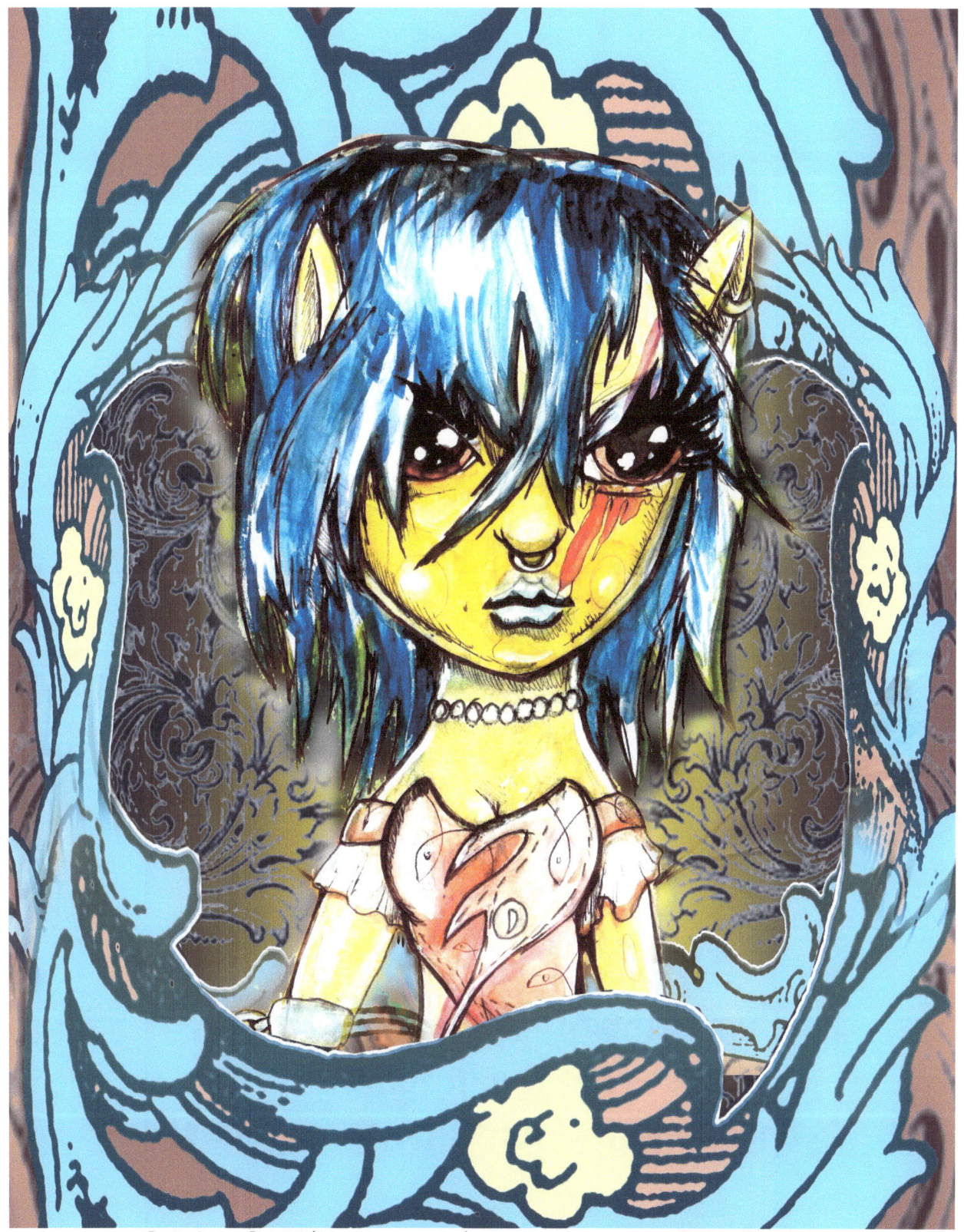

Punky by Ivy Patrick (ink and water color) = Graphic enhancement by Desiree Finkbeiner

Winter

Cutting winds and icy parts
frosty fingers, frozen hearts,
runny noses, chilly air.
Bundle up and hug a bear!
Froze in time, a thought gone past,
something to make a memory last.
Hope of warmth to start a fire,
in the thawing heart, desire.
Snowflakes, heartaches, icy breath,
fending off the fear of death.
Snuggle up to keep us warm,
outside rages up a storm.
Patience dear, winter will pass
and in the spring come up the grass.
Melt away the snow and ice,
until the air is warm and nice.
Pass away the gloomy skies,
and bring the sunshine to my eyes!

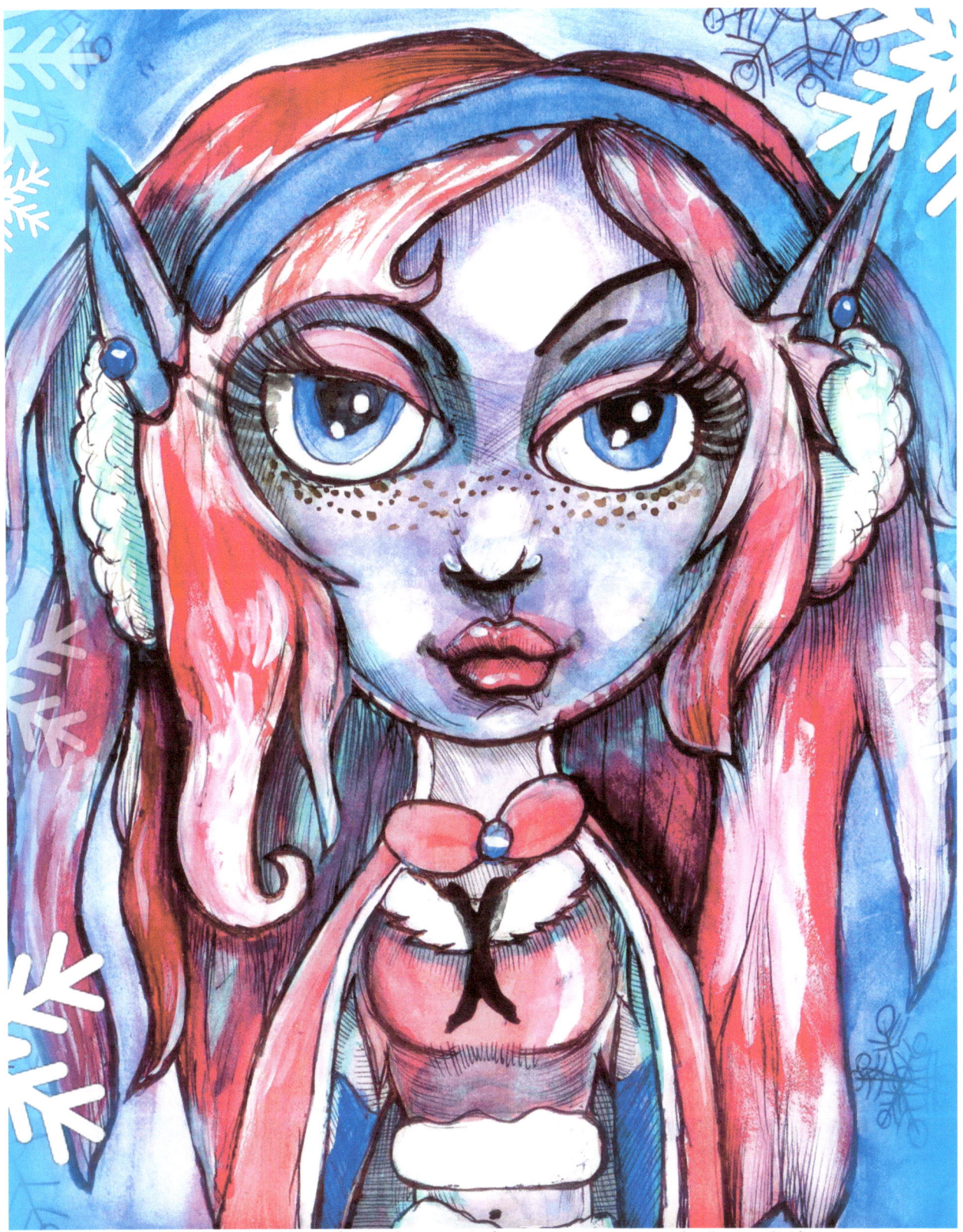

Winter Fairy by Ivy Patrick (ink and water color) = Graphic enhancement by Desiree Finkbeiner

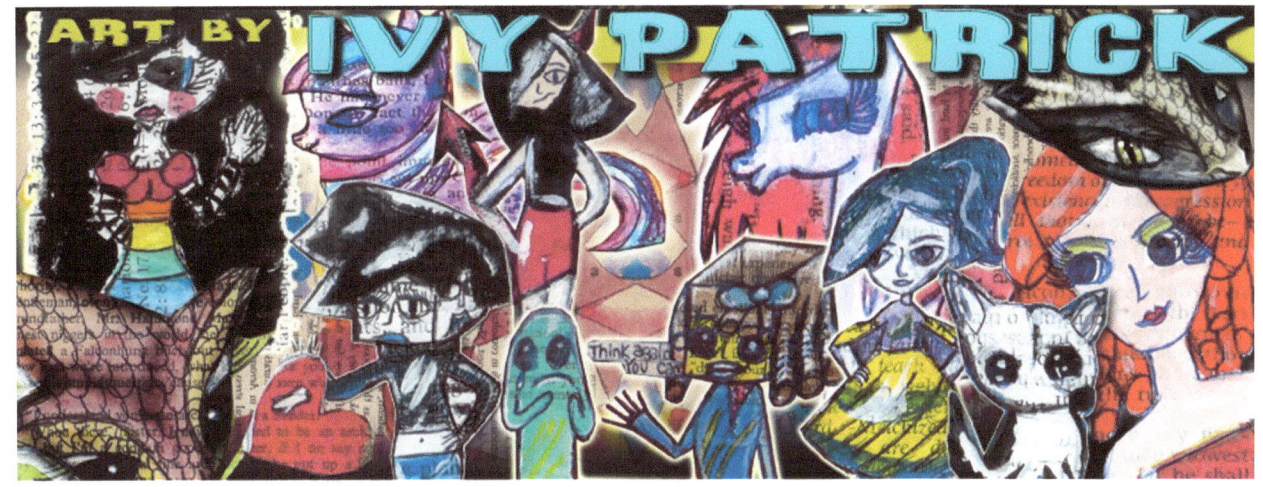

About the Illustrator

Ivy Patrick has been selling her at since she was 4 years old, following the creative path of her mother, who has encourage Ivy to embrace her own artistic voice. And Ivy has done just that! Her art captures hearts all over the world and continues to amaze and inspire. Her work was first published at the age of 6 in a commissioned children's book, and she wrote her first chapter book at the age of 8. This book is her debut feature with many more to come!

At the time of this book's publication (2015) Ivy was 10 years old. She hopes to publish many more books!

Ivy Patrick

facebook.com/pages/Ivy-Patrick/156799614385183 (Facebook Fan Page)

stores.ebay.com/Fink-Art-Studio (for original art and licensed products)

society6.com/finkartstudio (for Ivy's art on licensed products)

Please LIKE and FOLLOW to see what's next!

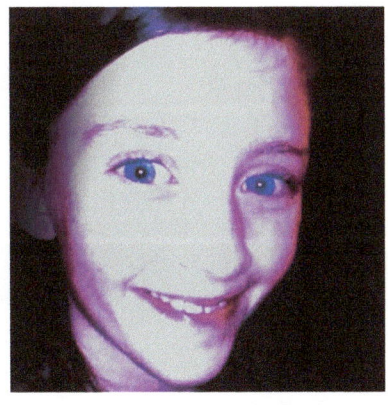

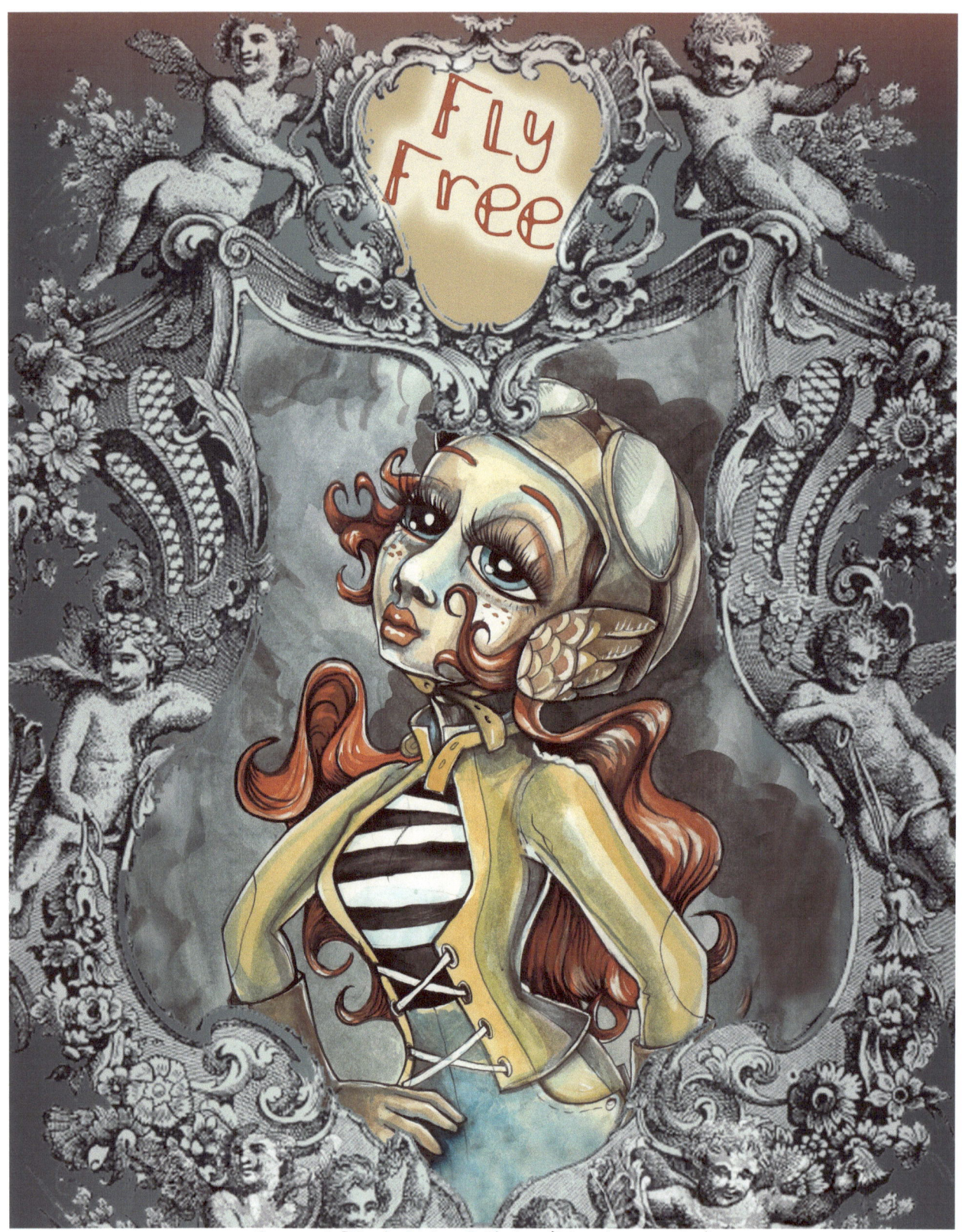

Steampunk Pilot by Desiree Finkbeiner (ink and water color)

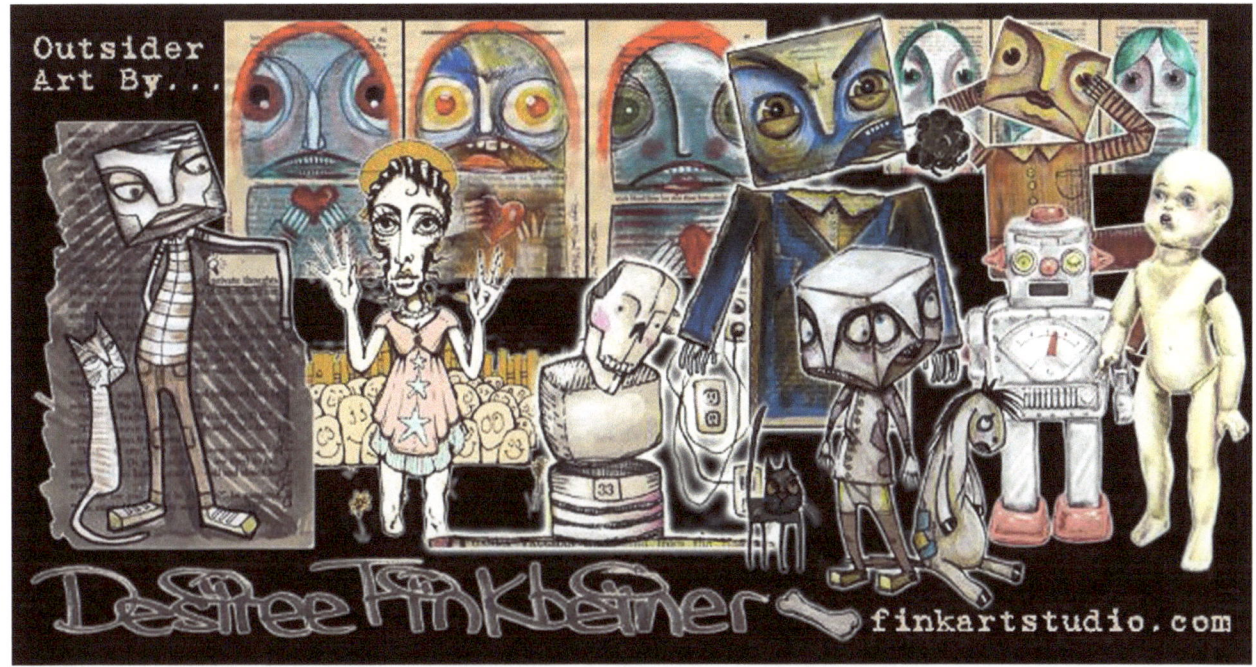

Outsider Art By...

finkartstudio.com

About the Author (Poetry in this book)

Desiree began her artistic journey at a very young age. By the time she was 22 she had written hundreds of songs, released 7 studio albums and performed over 300 live shows in 11 states with various musical acts; all this while pursuing an art degree. After obtaining her degree, she left the music industry to focus on art, business and family. Her original award-winning art is collected world-wide and she's written several books, among them a best-selling series. Desiree is the proud mother of Ivy Patrick, thrilled to see Ivy follow in her artistic and industrious footsteps. Nothing makes her happier than to see her children blossom and embrace their own artistic voices!

Desiree Finkbeiner

finkartstudio.com (for official archives, biography and galleries)

facebook.com/finkartstudio (for art/writing related news only)

stores.ebay.com/Fink-Art-Studio (for original art and licensed products)

amazon.com/author/desireefinkbeiner (for books on Amazon)

Please LIKE and FOLLOW to see what's next!

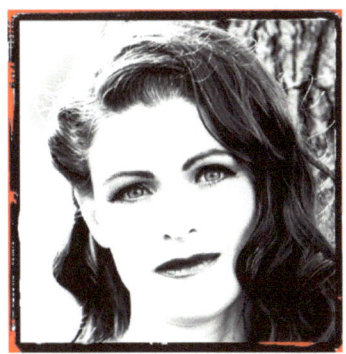

www.ingramcontent.com/pod-product-compliance
Lightning Source LLC
Chambersburg PA
CBHW050407180526
45159CB00005B/2176